Buried in the Margins

poems by

Kelsi Folsom

Finishing Line Press
Georgetown, Kentucky

Buried in the Margins

ACKNOWLEDGMENTS

These poems were first published in the following journals, to whose editors
I hold the deepest gratitude:

The Caribbean Writer - "Proud Faces," ""Landlines"
Desert Willow Press - "The Nightgown"
Voice of Eve - "Breath," "Daughter of Eve," "Berries and Ponies"
Voices de la Luna - "Mariachi Postcards," "Heartbeats"
borrowed solace - "Cantaloupes," "The Cake I Didn't Want to Eat"
        (formerly titled "Ambition")

Publisher: Leah Maines
Editor: Christen Kincaid
Cover Art: Hope Olson
Author Photo: Wesley Folsom
Cover Design: Elizabeth Maines McCleavy

Printed in the USA on acid-free paper.
Order online: www.finishinglinepress.com
        also available on amazon.com

Author inquiries and mail orders:
Finishing Line Press
P. O. Box 1626
Georgetown, Kentucky 40324
U. S. A.

Table of Contents

For every woman whose heart is buried somewhere—may the wild beauty and persistent mercy of Jesus resurrect you.

For my parents—your dedicated love never misses an opportunity to walk alongside of your children.

For W—you always come back.

Breath

Mingling,
our journeys;
The ones we have taken
and
the ones yet to be took...

The resonance of varied spirits
colors our walk,
asking and telling,
nodding and dreaming,
weaving
so grandly
their unifying threads...

stories;

The ones we can tell
and
The ones we cannot.

Revelation collides with mystery
and
(sometimes)
words
Become
flesh.

Part I

Mariachi Postcards

Tacos at La Gloria lit a match.
With a shot of tequila,
eyes glowed and rain poured,
pink and orange filling up the river.

A gracious refrain of mariachi
and lights etched like scratch 'n' sniffs
bleary and bright, glowing like
fireflies drunk in the night.

A sight for sore eyes
is your hand on my thigh
as we drink and dream
under the low Texas sky.

The rose, do you see it?
stone cold, stone faced
romancing each passerby,
come, have a look!

See, she is nursing
the wounds of a nation,
this little flower here,
come and pray,
come and pray.

Part your lips with the departed,
singing heaven's song on earth,
crying, peace be still and find your rest
right back where you began.

Stars kissing limestone,
love giving birth.
Brassy observations
set the tone for the night,
a fiesta of paletas and confetti.

Here, by the river,
walking by the river,
forever by the river all the feet
of many colors find their futures
at the mouth of stone and water.

Sea-Blue Eyes

My love,
your eyes enrapture my existence,
                insistent,
Your love beckons me beyond resistance.
        (exuberantly)
My soul is laid out before you
        (unbound)
to be wound with the fibers of you.

Only you,
focused
intently on me.

Desire and passion,
I feel
and
I see.

Your gaze is speaking,
my spirit knows, grows
and so leaping I'm
caught in the throes:

The kind,
      the gentle,
           the loving,
      the laughing,
the giving,
      unending adventure
          of striving.

I'm diving into all that is you,
        (immersed)
Steady in your glorious eyes
        of sea- blue.

Daughter of Eve

I am the fragment of a rib,
                    cracked,
                    reborn,
laid forth to be bare,
split wide to hold
wanting and sorrow.

From fractured embraces,
I emerged, yawning,
a marinated embodiment
of horror
and need

but look,

as the light comes,
I will be:
frosted ruminations
of practice
and peace.

I am chewing the seder of aggravations,
splashing in the spit of its ripest fruits.

Amidst clipping the sprigs
of rosemary shoulders,
I dust fragrant fears
off many calloused feet.

Behold this womb
of laughter and dreams
seated at the table for eternity.

Cantaloupes

The white veined skin takes me back to the aisle
where I stand seeking respite from the blazing Texas heat.

On the prowl with my mom,
pride and glamour on the hunt.

I am only five, but I know the ropes:
a knock on its belly,

a sniff of its rear, this one here
because it's fragrant at the ends.

The slip of the flesh peeling wet from the knife
takes me back to a patio with prosciutto

and wine and my father seated savoring
fruit wrapped in swine, a divine

conversation of juice and sunshine.
I am only eight, but I sit among the greats

who knew the romance of Italian melons.
The tender refrain of first love fills my mouth

with each desperate incision of hunger and softness,
stirring up nightcaps and cards in the lounge,

a symphony of stars swooning hard over Tel Aviv,
a seduction so subtle and yet, he doesn't love me,

I know, but at sixteen,
isn't it nice to dream?

The squelch of the seeds takes me back to a beach
where the waters paw the sand,

lips meeting golden hands

warm and rough, sloughing through

to softened skin upended
singing, "I'm a seahorse,

no, a mermaid, island goddess
of the waves," every morning

wrapping fruit with meat,
he loves me and I love him,

finally flying here, complete
at twenty-seven.

Cleaved

I. *At the Stove*

The sound of cooking is just like a kiss:
sizzling, tempered, and timed.

Sometimes it's smoking,
sometimes it's simmering,

either way,
spoons will be licked.

II. *On the Table*

Freshly cut cantaloupe
winks in the sunlight,

juicy,
wet,
tender.

Sweet flesh begs
to melt inside your
mouth, breaking down
in foamy mastication.

III. *Bananas*

Peel back the skin like a jacket,
each flap revealing white flesh,

sturdy and soft,
firm in my grasp,

popping the tip
in the seal of my lips.

IV.   A *Dash of Nutmeg*

Sex is a stolen moment
melting on the freezer,
sitting on the edge of ice,
laughing 'cause they'll
never know the
things the spices do.

Unmentionables

Did I mention silk
is my favorite grace?
Leavers of lace lay
flat against soft skin,
weaving elegant dreams
and innocent fights
like gin flirting quietly
beneath the moonlight,
nestled clear and gentle,
rocking through the night.

Fly Me to the Moon

Thighs are open,
breath is quickened.

Bodies meld,
desire thickened.

I see your face,
such bliss and peace.

My mind a reverie
of should and would

and can't, and won't,
a simple wish:

to be there where you are.

New Birth

I lost more
of my mind than I did
my hair
when you first came out,
water-logged and anxious,
a bit like your mother.

I cared little
for social graces
and faces appearing
to peck at the chores
and leave leftovers
at my door.

I needed sleep
like a memory foam bra
lifting my pelvic floor
and remembering
where the keys
to my sex drive ran off to.

Dear Baby Daddy

You are a wonderful man.
My french press is always clean.
The dishes are only half dirty.
My food will never spoil in the fridge.

My hips will never be lonely.
My cheeks think they rule the world.
My legs might as well be Betty Grable's,
and my breasts might as well be Pam Anderson's.

I like inhabiting your reality,
the one that is ripe and inviting;
the one that didn't push out humans
while morphine dripped into her veins,

the one that still finds love-making exciting.

A Matter of Patience

I don't know any secrets,
I just forgot the time.
Like the time I cried when
I drug my newborn into Starbucks
by myself and there were no
seats and no strangers willing to
concede their comfort to me:
a vacant womb expunged of its life
and searching longingly for a good reason
why this carseat breaks my spoiled arms,
and takes, for the life of me, so much time
I didn't know I had until I couldn't find it.

Part II

Good Morning

Give your children
the pages of your heart.

Let them doodle
and color and paint

and push aside
everything taking up

pencils and pens,

and write all the stories,
like squirrels on cocaine.

Am I a Writer?

I'm just not sure…
I tire of bearing witness,
lugging stories on my back.

It's a hat not quite fitting
my large, bent head
crunching words all day

like a shredder too full:
change the trash or it jams,

proving useless.

The Cake I Didn't Want to Eat

We slip into our comforts
so easily, honestly, their
arms enfolding grab
a hold of name-less
empties wallowing on
the bottom floor.

have you been there?

The basement of your soul,
I mean, the portico of
wasted dreams, a steaming
pile of should-have-beens,
the sediment of sparkling
goals you left out
on the counter?

It's gross and cold,
but surprisingly well lit.

Grab a scone and settle
in, read the lists of
reasons why, all the
life you purposed,
can't be had today.

Rum Punch

What am I drinking?
I'll give you one guess:
the frayed disrespect
standing sentient to my left,
eating buckets of popcorn,
the bag behind a door closed
                    on purpose,
                    on repeat,
                    repeated
                    on purpose:
keep the door closed,
                    Shut the door,
don't open it,
                    I've told you before!
But, honestly, really,
what do they know?
You can't wrangle
immaturity
from a tightened bow.

Mommeee

What is it about the vowel "e"?
How does it communicate
more effectively than "a"?

What is it telling me
that you haven't
already said?

Does the length of
your cry mean
you mean it this time?

Like a lasso flung
around the corner,
this vowel
spins a noose around my neck
back to you,

and you hold it,
tugging me out
from the quiet shade
of my selfish life,
as I rush to your side
to ask, "what?"

Peals of Laughter

At some point,
it all becomes noise;
even the good,
noise.

To Be Three

I. *Confidence*

She pushes wind
aside with every step,
straightening her sunglasses,
clutching her purse,
announcing her presence
with every bounce of her curls.

II. *Tantrums*

She splits my brain in half,
                    seething,
hurling pointed cries,
                and shaking,
eyes bugging out of her skull,
                and making,
misunderstood
HEARD.
            But, I'm listening.
            Doesn't she know?

III. *Instinct*

When will they learn
to use words instead
of tears to have
an opinion and
step over their fears?

IV. *Exuberance*

Observe a sunflower
and smile
at the resemblance
sunny, yellow petals
have with

a little girl
who is three.

Both need
adoration
and vitamin D,
survival their
ability to receive.

V.   *The Nightgown*

Pilled pleats neatly tucked inside the hem.
Coiling up like curls bouncing just above her knees.

She doesn't know they hold her together,
red and gentle, washed and worn.

They lay beside her dreams at night,
quick to fly at morning's breach
of bright insistence telling her to eat.

The Request

Blue eyes so hopeful,
open like porcelain teacups
right before the teapot's trunk
unfurls its steaming depths.

Poised like a learned lion,
tensely coiled for her capture
awaiting silently
one candid movement.

Shocking tendrils
spiral away from
her upturned face,
a mile a minute
her varying assessments
play across her gaze.

tread carefully

they read, like
a vintage magazine
yellowing at the edges.

This is the end
or the beginning,
depending on your words.

Snacktime with Toddlers

Your hands make me nervous,
what happens next?
Another dream ripped away,
                    (laid to rest)
or burned instead,
dripping over coals
like marshmallows
à la Dalí?

I want to be left alone,
yet I'm desperate to be seen,
but for all the unknowns,
I think   *(I know)*
I'm glad you're next to me.

Strands

My hair is heavy
like my lot in life.
I brush it,
coating the strands
with oil and sunshine
and still it leaves,
like a herd of goats
gathering beneath
the mint mat stuck
to the bottom
of the mint bathtub
to keep my kids from
slipping under the tepid
bathwater. I feed it
with folic acid and
colorful fruits, coaxing
the roots with massage
and rosemary.

Still, it would rather
leave my scalp
than burrow deeper
brown and fancy
to sway wild
in the wind.

Getting Ready

The wood,
a bit more green,
and slick,
reminds me
I've forsaken
all persuasions
and occasions
fitting wearing
certain jewelry.

The ebony triangles,
dimpled with age,
recommend two different
outfits I could take the
town in, pay back the
darkness I've subjected
them to. It's vain,
but they don't deserve
this mossy coating
of neglect.

Date Night

The ice is thick
beneath my skates,
winter's breath has
paved the way
when cracks
like glaciers
punch the inlines
toppling my footing.

I'm furious the unexpected has bested me again.

I grab your hand
and squeeze it tighter,
this time I am more
prepared to carve an edge
and tiptoe lighter
skirting around the fence.

Dinner now, ensconced
in J. Crew, looking
hot perusing through
the cocktail list, I'll have
the blackberry mojito.

Sip. Silence. chew chew,
fold the napkin, stroke
a hem, I don't know, what
do you want to talk about?

Cut your steak a little deeper,
ask a question like you're here.
Sometimes I think we're just not meant to be,
Then I step away from the mirror.

Small Talk

Do you see them dancing,
egging each other on?
They flirt and tease
and ease their pain
with trickery masked
as waltzing.

I thought we knew
each other better.

On Listening

When you refuse to
look reality in the
eye, you can fabricate
all kinds of half-truths
that make you sound
like you're the only
one who's clued in,
all puffed up like the
microwave's experiment
with the marshmallows.

BOOM

It's a mess.
Now who's the fool?

Deference

Malachi 2:10

We want so badly
for there to be
a right side and
a wrong side,
but mostly,
there are just sides,
independent of the others
though sometimes they
clasp a shoulder
or poke toes
in the same dirt
drawing the same boundaries
in the same sand
the hands of time
already claimed.

What does it mean
to condescend the breath
inside of another?

It all came from God,
so we're all notes
from the same lungs.

Evening

Do I start with the man,
                    or you?
Do I start with the room,
                    or the view?
Do I start with the moment
            my hand
                met your chest
            and made
                        peace with the pain,
            or the
                few moments left
            that we
        made
of the dark
        and the rain?

Part III

Resistance

No,
I'm not ready
to leave.

Look around,
the tears tell a different story,
the rain fills the cistern
one storm at a time
until slowly,
very slowly
one truth spills out:

Friends make everything better,
even the sorrow.

It is too rich to bear,
too impeccable to imagine
the height and depth and
breadth of friendship borne
out of adversity.

These eyes and energies
with a finger on our pulse,
lighting fire to our struggles
knowing the flames
will keep us warm.

Tea on the front porch,
glass art and painting,
wine on a stone bench
exhausting the ocean's glances
just a short walk from home.

No,
I'm not ready
to leave.

Moving Again

Tomorrow we leave,
already our hopes are packed back up,
a perfect freeze on memories
languishing in tandem.

Storage is too small a word
for what I've kept and had and learned;
a space to lay in state for months,
dreaming of a grand return.

The Garage Sale

Oh how I miss the "perfect egg-pan,"
sold unbeknownst to me
to a stranger at a price
far beneath its worth.

The pan that served omelettes
everyday and breakfast tacos,
sustaining our first year
of marriage and pregnancy,

Gone.

It was just a pan,
but,
just a pan
brought us life.

Those letters scribed
with soul drenching words,
words that would uproot
weeds from a weary heart.

Letters like food in the
yellowed beaks of ravens
brimming warm for
a prophet long ago,

Gone.

They were just paper,
but,
just paper
brought me hope.

Little outfits chosen
to nuzzle fat cheeks,
little spaces curated

in love:

a bathtub, a napper,
a crib and a stroller,
a walker, a playmat,
control, like a false sense,

Gone.

They were just things,
but,
just things
brought me home.

Seasons change,
and mine go quick,
often without fanfare
or memorial.

Their graves surface in old pictures,
like moments,
frozen inside ice cubes
of breath.

Sailing Ships

She thinks her ship
has sailed already,
thrown an anchor
in the rising tide,
waving at the waves
like she couldn't
grab the wheel
that's for women
like me
whose time is now,
or at least
pretends to be.

Proud Faces

I don't want to write,
the ink is too flat.
I closed the curtains for the last time.
How does one write about that?

The dreams and fears tangled up in the fabric
blowing with the stuttered breath of soursop
and madness, they can't be accounted for,
they already came and went.

I left salt in the soil, though I
prayed more for fruit, patient
promises for feisty children,
harvesting the dirt.

We struggled so much,
raking rock after rock,
clawing mold out of our eyes
and beans into our throats.

Now we see oak trees,
proud faces of creation,
aging magistrates of wonder,
running circles around the time.

Have you looked at an oak tree?
traced it's barnacled veins
through the sky?
Offering to detox the blood of
broken mothers cleaved to man,
children, pride,
and country,
everything but themselves.

Hot Flash

Women are tired.
Tired of defense.
Tired of permission,
Tired of dismissal.

Show me a woman
who has not known abuse
who has not been betrayed
who has not been manipulated
who has not been coerced
into unspeakable things:

taking the fall,
writing the letters,
harboring secrets
to stay in the game.

Such oppression and anger,
hatred and fear,
selfishness and ego,
patronizing the years.

All the world is heaving,
spitting,
bursting with disfunction,
hurling
insults left and right,
like they are little boys
with tiny guns

fight with your heart,
not your might.

I see the bonds of ancient evils
loosened even though it's hotter,
seven times, to be exact.

I think God must be coming

soon.

Part IV

Indigenous Alien

It's so loud here;
the distant hum of traffic,
the grumble of lawn equipment.

The sun seems so far away,
and I am swallowed up
by land and bigness.
Feeling like an immigrant
in my own country,
though I was born here,
not made.

I never thought the ocean
would come to be a bridge.
I feel lost in America,
overlooked by modernity
and busy-ness,
and regulations,
and rules.

I miss humanity swept up in the
simplicity of working out
its truth with breath
and humble beginnings,
Not oppressed by a life
they don't have to live.

You can
            put the phone down
            pull the door shut
            laugh at absurdity
            drug the unknown.

Twin Engines

They think
their Dad
lives on
a plane.

Preposterous,
because only
the rich
would eat.

Both propellers
clear their
throats at
the birds

like a
gentle reminder
we fly
where eagles
dream. But,

what do
they know?
Their brains
are outside
them. What

happens when
the pressure
drops and
a wing
catches fire?

No one tells a bird what to do.

"Bye-bye, Dada,"
they wave

and point,
believing their
Maker will
hear them.

Landlines

The ring of a landline
strikes fear in my heart.
What news does it bring?
Are we falling apart?

I'm laying on my bed
clutching breaths
like flotation devices
while the wind whips
the tin roof with tree limbs
and fury, moaning loud
and strong with grievances
from the neck of Africa.

Maybe a mother is wailing
for her kidnapped child.
Maybe a father is dying
for some pride or a job,
anything
to fill the
gnaw
of starvation,
so sighs
fill the sky,
bearing down
like a Category 5.

Missing You

These bones keep me from you,
stretching sinews like yarn
needles wagging their
tails and finishing lace.

Lace, so delicate
but not quite true,
just a cobweb of cotton and time
like the sunsets I watch without you.

My chest was cut from you,
just for you,
a perfection of blood
and rhythm.

A cavity emptied
cries out in the void
bearing the image of its equal:

you.

Pulling Up the Sheets

Warm me,
in your distance
gather near me
with your thoughts
steer your heart towards
gentle burning
if you dare.

Warm me,
pleasant spring
eternal
drinking up
the nightclouds
with your fierce flirtation
pin me to the stars.

The Nightshift

It's painful the
wrinkles these sheets
leave without you;
yawning and folding
over themselves as
you while away
an education abroad.

I thought loving you
meant going with you.
I never imagined staying.

Separate Beds

I missed your call and
I'm angry. This box
of technology didn't
deliver the magic
of pixels, time,
and speed, the
keeper of your face
kept quiet instead.

I'm pissed.

I've grown accustomed to
convenience, and this
little blip takes
a dump on the
little flame my
heart keeps for you.

Even the sunflowers
won't look me in the eye.

I feel distant,
am I wrong to?
I didn't smile much today
but my heart is full,
I suppose.

I have not seen your body
in weeks, you're my husband.
I have a right to you, and yet

here we are in separate beds,
              different time zones,
              different days,
              our marriage
buried in the margins.

Loneliness

An owl hoots outside
the window by himself.

I mimic his cry
for company wrought
from nothing else

but shared dreams
and equal suffering,

a partner for his song.

Panic Attack

A ghastly horror grips my core,
A thousand tears and traumas
tore
sore
were they to be trapped so long,
waiting for courage to be sent to swine
no longer twined inside my mind.

Darkness pounds against my chest
heating up fear
to sneer and snarl
and yank up
rusty anchors
staid
still
within
my heart.

A taste of hell,
truly hell,
a white hot sorrow
fells my joy,
Will I shatter? Will I drown?

but wait,

a glimmer shimmers through,
a golden melody of truth,
a hand sent down for rescue,
just to rescue me
and set me free.

Wrapped in light
and
Kept in love,
Holding tight to hope
for I believe

I AM
made well again,
and daily
and at night.

Ghosts of Christmases Past

The lights are tangled,
cozy and confused,
plastic eyes once
shining bright,
brazen beacons
of ancient text
leading the shepherds
to the holy child.

Now they're coiled,
like a pile of
dead snakes,
eyes vacant,
dust gathering
in the corners.

Each year I think
we'll find the end,
and know which
light got broken.

Spines

The rosemary bush spreads
her fingers to find me.
I linger in her piny breath,
hoping restitution climbs each rung
of brittle vertebrae
biding time
and
slinging burdens,
just like Santa Claus
on Christmas Eve,
big bag bursting with
new songs of peace
filling space where
doubts and gravity
once compressed me.

Respite

The rosemary is dying; I hope it's not a sign.
Burnt eyelashes crinkled like fairy dust,
but it's death, a humiliation of what it was born to do.

I read somewhere that this bush is where Mary laid
her mantle to rest, so the needles became blessed by
the hope that she found in a moment of stopping.

sweet, sticky, glorious stopping.

Part V

Adaptation

The sun hits the road
like a code to be cracked,
taunting the pavement
with blistering heat.

Listen up, gravel,
I'll give you the facts:
Never forget that you're
under my feet.

Vision of the Ancients

I see mothers of the ages,
of all cultures, of all times,
carrying torches,
lighting the darkness,
soothing the future
with hummed lullabies.

They carve their way in beautiful strength
with faith and song, waiting....watching....warding...waiting...
staying the course with never-ending grace.

Oh how God's heart opens for mothers!
How tenderly he wipes their brows and lifts their faces—

cradling weariness in his well-worn presence,
sweet rocking back and forth
along the curving river's edge.

Revel in the favor you were born for,

dear mother, sweet dignity,
take your place, wait and see.

Keep walking, your song is growing,
not fading like some would say.
Carve the silence with your love and light.
Rise again, be healed, empowered.

You,

like soft silk sliding
down from skin exposed,
unfurl your holy breath,
lifting each earnest desire.

Stalwarts of elegance,
extend your hands,

don your mantles
and dance.

You're a glory to behold
when your bruises come unbound.

At the Botanical Gardens

The sunlight shares
its fruit with the
patient, and the
eager find their
seat in the shade
of desire, pointing
fingers, grinning
greedy as the harvest
turns its bed.

Have you tilled
the land your
feet take,
treading lightly
trails of honor?

All who have
walked before say,
"Come,
this is the way."

Berries and Ponies

The shadow of her youth
wiped her brow as she
bent over strawberries elbowing their way
out of hot soil and garbage bags.

Colored hair and french tips
couldn't hide the years she's
cultivated beauty from the
wild earth, and smiled at her lot.

Look in her eyes and
see her hung around
the neck of a pony,
bareback and free,
sheets flying in the wind.

The orchard her playground,
the world still so small,
curls bouncing like the berries
in her basket wouldn't fall.

She's a mother,
three times over now,
still tilling earth's potential,
never knowing when
the seeds she's sowing

might be her last.

To Korea With Love (after Min Jin Lee's *Pachinko*)

The mountains are tired,
presiding over furrowed
brows and scrambling
to make amends with
simple beginnings.

(remember we are dust,
bright particles from the ground)

Have you heard?
You're beautiful.
Look at the shadows
of your verdant hills,
brushing shoulders with the ocean.

Look how lovely this
flame in your heart
reaching wide for
a name that's all yours.

all yours.

I want to embrace you
eye to eye, mouth to mouth
with spoonfuls of *kimchi*
your great *umma* made,

Press my cheek
to your brow,
raise my chest to
your hand,
kissing callouses
and withered bones
gloved inside
a weathered
love of man,
mother,
and country.

Consider the Dirt

People have forgotten
how to love their land.
Press a cheek
to the dirt
and just breathe.

Land.

listen

You might hear
a story trapped
atop the earth's diaphragm.

It would have drowned
had you not
found her mouth,
Looked inside
and
wondered why
green
keeps on growing
in spite of
neglect?

Unborn

If you want to grow in me,
have your way.
But I'd prefer if
you came another day.

My house is broken,
but you can try and
have your cake,
maybe eat it too.

Perhaps, there's more to be made.

Part VI

Marvel

It was the scalpel at midnight
that plead my case,
a jury scrubbed up,
snouts bridled for war.

Today, yes.
Today's a good day to cry,
pull the stop on those lungs
and just wail.

Reach wide and far,
therein lies your heart:
the thin place between
you and me.

Waiting in Terminal B

The automatic doors
open and close like
it's freaking Star Wars
and I'm Leia with
a wookie at my back.

Corridors, white
corridors and acrid smells
accosting every pore
of skin to wake me
up to now with you
in front of me.

A gush of tears
mingles with the pungent
scent of traveling and
delays and loafers
clopping along to cell
phone calls and aderrall
for strung out children
bouncing off the walls.

The Baggage Claim

I'm nervous to see you.
Will our bodies remember?
It's been one hundred days
and I've made a life
without you.

We each have our part,
it's true, we do talk
on the fringes of our day
and I thought we might make
of it, more than we have.

It's weird to crowd the distance
like reaching long and sweating
over fat bales of hay,
convinced,
the stretching might
indeed fan us to flame.

But I'm game,
if you are,
I'm ready,
if you are,
I'm trying,
if you are,

to once again become
the same.

Heartbeats

How could my cells remember the smell
of raisin bran and whole milk,
the audience of disorder and pickled
doubts growing in my womb?

The sterile care of screens
and injections watering
a small root of salvation
or two, since they multiplied

and now here I am,
hooked up and hemorrhaging,
hoping my body can save you
and me, so we wait.

Yes, we wait for the time
to wield its salve
at 30 weeks and
cut you out,

one at a time,
two by two,

and place you
safe and sound
and screaming
comfortably against

my skin.

Heartbeats humming
ta-dum, ta-dum, ta-dum.
Heartbeats remembering
here is where I belong.

While at a Cabin in Dripping Springs

I know,
spaghetti and meatballs,
how original!

But have you
breathed a sigh
twining pasta up

in tines of silver
passed between your
fingers like a

salsa in Havana?

It's 5pm,
the time when
clouds forget which way

they're going, stop
and marvel at the
honeyed sunbeams

drooling on the table?

And love,
freshly shaved,
is seated softly

to your right,
he inhales loud
and long, you

exhale picking
up right where
he left off.

Chew, chew, chew,

look around
and swallow,

savoring the ground beef
drenched in basil,
donned with peppercorn

spooning with the noodles.

So mundane, this
meal of everyday
that two-steps off your plate.

But you've never been
more warm and bright
while sitting next to fate.

Cultivated

I'm ready to be food,
bread and wine,
broken manna,
split and seeded
with the dirt of healing,
flowering anew.

Hands

I can do
anything
if your hand
is in mine,
casting
shadows on
my legs
as we
walk an impossible
line
between have
and have not,
casting lots
with the sky,
wringing love
from every
hand me down
steam pressed
and alive.

Hill Country Summer

It's perfectly hot today.
My skin prickles
like when I pull a
steaming casserole of
shredded potatoes, bacon,
and cheese from the oven
but I've taken a moment to pause
before the door opens all
the way to release it's fury
upon me. I've stood aside,
breathing patiently, maybe
drooling a little at the fats
now fully cooked, mitted hands
relaxed into the drawing out
of food. Ah yes. Perfect.

This heat knows its place,
like it's been trained away from
nuisance. It dries the juice dripping
hungrily from my chin, having
pierced the skin of a fuzzy, fragrant
peach, while cicadas are rattling
into their wings,
relishing the smack
of 90 degrees,
there's no better time
for dancing and iced tea.

It's perfect.

The Golden Afternoon

I love the way the sun sits
in the afternoon

easy.

Each cloud a lazy boy
dispersing muted rays
on the horizon.

I love how simple
an afternoon is—
no pressure, no mayhem,

just cicadas and hot tea,
the promises of the day
just blossoming to fulfillment

like steam climbing
up into enlightenment.

The Great Unwinding

Hope abounds in plenty,
I wash in it,
cleansing myself,
delighting in its
beautiful fragrance.

How wonderful is
the bouquet of
second chances,
to be soft again,
to be listening well,

to be stronger.

Kelsi Folsom is a Texas-born writer, whose work is published in *The Caribbean Writer, West Texas Literary Review, Women Who Live on Rocks, Knocked Up Abroad, borrowed solace, Voice of Eve,* and *Motherly.* Having lived most recently in the Dutch Caribbean, she is here for rum punch, creole art, and *soca* music. She's fascinated by contradictions, in-spired by unusual architecture, and obsessed with the duality of surface to simultaneously conceal and reveal the truth of a matter, which she wrestles with in her chapbook, *Words the Dirt Meant to Share* (Desert Willow Press, 2018).

For awhile she put her B.M. in Voice Performance from Anderson University to good use, traveling the world participating in operas, jazz bands, musicals, church services, and choirs, but then she had three kids and needed to trade in her audition heels for a laptop and black coffee. When she's not writing or wrangling children, she explores other cultures with her family, contributes regularly to *Red Tent Living Magazine*, a faith based online women's publication, scours estate sales, pretends she can sew, works as an Independent Ambassador for Noonday Collection (a fair-trade fashion and accessories brand providing economic opportunity for vulnerable communities worldwide), dates her husband, and performs wherever she can, most recently with OPERA San Antonio. You can follow her writing and activities at www.kelsifolsom.com and on IG @kelsifolsom.

www.ingramcontent.com/pod-product-compliance
Lightning Source LLC
Chambersburg PA
CBHW021152090426
42740CB00008B/1061